Increased Profitability Through Quality Customer Service

ISBN 0 9521137 1 6

PRINTED BY M S LITHO

Acknowledgements

City Promotions would like to thank the following people for their help with the production of this guide:

Paul Gibson – Author
formerly of Harrods & House of Fraser

Alexander R. Watt – For the Foreword
Director, Customer Services Europe, Dun & Bradstreet Europe

IDM Ltd – For allowing advance access to their customer service software, eXerlin

Nathan Skinner – The cartoonist

Kim Coomber – Researcher and Editor
Marketing Manager, IDM

Acknowledgements

FOREWORD

The current business climate is such that no company can afford to be complacent in its dealings with its customers. Competition is always present and will be quick to step in and sign up a disgruntled customer.

At Dun & Bradstreet in the 80's we began to face increased competition in Europe and recognised that, not only did our systems have to change, but, more importantly, we had to adopt a customer related culture involving our associates at all levels.

Much of what we had to do was common sense. A customer culture means putting yourself in the customer's shoes and performing to meet his/her expectations.

However, to many the process is painful. Old habits die hard and there is a tendency to think in terms of what you *can* do rather than what the customer expects. Also, some associates find it difficult to relate to the external customer and tend not to understand the key rôle they play in the process.

Quality programmes abound. But in the end, it is the involvement of associates, at whatever level, to determine how he or she can improve the process, which differentiates one company from another.

Above all, keep it simple. This booklet does just that whilst embodying the key thought process which, if followed up, will improve your image with the customer.

At Dun & Bradstreet we have seen massive improvements in Quality and Service since we adopted the "Customer Culture". What is more important, our customers have noticed it too. Follow the basic principles set out in this booklet and your customers will also see the change.

Alexander R. Watt
Director, Customer Services – Europe
D&B Europe Ltd

CONTENTS

Introduction . . . . Page 1

What is Customer Service? . . . . Page 5

What are the Benefits? . . . . Page 13

The Customer . . . . Page 17

The Service . . . . Page 23

The Staff . . . . Page 27

"Perceptions", "Expectations" and "Attitudes". . . Page 31

Measuring and Monitoring . . . . Page 39

Reactive Customer Service . . . . Page 45

Pro-active Customer Service . . . . Page 49

The Answer . . . . Page 57

Final Thoughts. . . . . Page 59

The Company Commitment . . . . Page 67

APPENDIX

The Ten Commandments
            and
The Seven Deadly Sins . . . . Page 69

Introduction

Introduction

Before you start to read this guide, there are some orientation guidelines which you need to bear in mind throughout.

Quality of Service is:

1. As much YOUR responsibility as anyone else's.

2. A direct reflection, in many instances, of how your company deals with a shortfall or under achievement caused by one or more of YOU.

3. Not achieved by few on behalf of many, it is achieved BY EVERYONE.

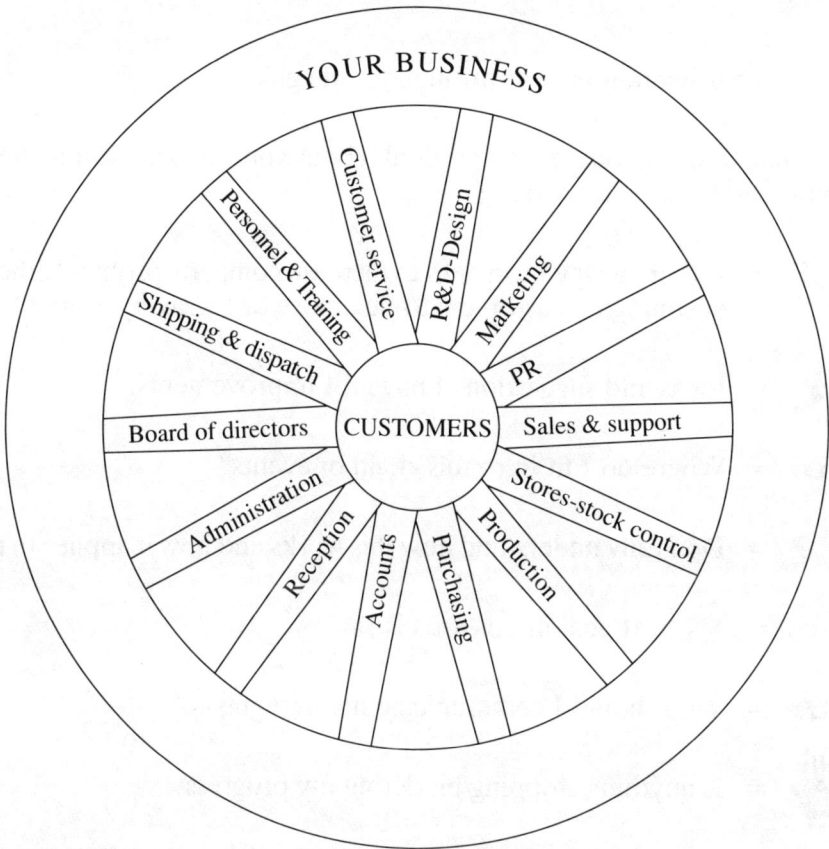

This diagram may not exactly fit the way your company is structured. However, the basis is applicable to any business.

Each area within your company represents a spoke. Just like a wheel, if one of these spokes fails, the wheel will collapse. A bumpy ride for everyone is the only possible outcome. Customers, after all, form the hub of your business and "Quality service cannot be achieved by few on behalf of many".

The following symbols appear throughout the guide.

Every time you find one, stop and think about your answer. It may help if you make notes as you go along.

£ = Is there a way I can help to increase company profits. Either by encouraging customers to buy more or by saving money?

⚡ = Ideas and suggestions I have for improvements.

⊂◻◻◻◻⊃ = Where do I fit in to this chain of events?

? = Do I fully understand how this works and how it applies to me?

◎ = My next goal in this area is . . .

☎ = Who should I communicate my thoughts to?

✋ = Is anything stopping/hindering my progress?

Whenever you find one of these symbols do not be afraid to write down the answers/suggestions you believe to be correct. There is space provided at the end of each chapter.

This is a practical guide for you. Your answers/suggestions will change regularly as products and customer requirements change. Keep track of new thoughts and understandings using this method.

This guide has been specifically designed to provoke thoughts and ideas. Used and reviewed regularly against current situations, it will prove an invaluable part of your strategy in the future.

What is Customer Service?

WHAT IS CUSTOMER SERVICE?

Let's start with the dictionary definitions:

CUSTOMER

: A person who buys goods or services

: A person with whom one has dealings

SERVICE

: An act of help or assistance

: The act or manner of serving guests, customers

SO – SIMPLY

Customer Service is the act of help or assistance for a person who buys.

If this sentence was as simple to perform as it is to write, then a guide, such as this would not be necessary.

However it is!

If I telephoned your company now, does the picture on the next page represent the sort of service I could expect?

If this simple cartoon can show so clearly the meaning of Customer Service, why should so many companies experience difficulties in providing this service to their customers?

Most companies are steeped in ideas, procedures, systems and practices that have been designed and implemented for the good of the company, and the employees. Generally, the customer comes a poor third on the list of people to consider.

Combine this with members of staff who are not aware that they can have an impact on the service provided. Add one or two errors of judgement and genuine mistakes, and now – just imagine for a moment you are the customer making contact with your company.

Are you certain you will be a satisfied customer, whatever the reason for your contact?

If the picture on the next page is a better representation of your company's approach to customer service then things need to change.

At this point it is fair to say that the quality of customer service provided by most companies falls between the two extremes.

However, I personally have experienced very close to both the top and the bottom end of this quality scale. If you think for just a few minutes about service experiences you have had, you may also recall similar encounters with service providers.

To work, the Customer Service culture should be a constantly evolving, interactive organism.

Consistently high quality results require:–

ENTHUSIASM

DEDICATION

and above all

AN UNDERSTANDING OF THE SERVICE REQUIRED BY YOUR CUSTOMERS

and
most importantly

THE FULL BACKING OF EVERYONE IN THE COMPANY.

Today's customers and consumers are the most demanding in history. They want better quality products and services, better value for money and the best possible treatment. Give it to them – only you and your colleagues can.

In the past when goods and services were less plentiful and options were few, customers were often resigned to, or did not expect anything other than indifference. Indifference will cost your company money and ultimately perhaps cost you your job!!

The highly competitive market place gives more options and choices with higher levels of service. If customers do not get this they go elsewhere and this has a direct effect on company profits.

£ – Is there a way I can increase profits?
♥ – Is anything stopping/hindering my progress?

Page 9

The company which recognises this higher customer expectation is a company to be reckoned with!

Delivering high levels of service, as part of the overall package when dealing with your customers, pays, and pays well. Remember,

‹"Indifference will cost your company money and ultimately perhaps, cost you your Job!!"›.

Creating and maintaining high quality customer service is, in principle, straightforward; Know what the customer wants and expects of you; be flexible in meeting those demands and work hard to make it easy for them to do business with you.

This approach is easy enough to describe but unless the right attitude is adopted by all, it is very difficult to achieve. Remember "Quality service cannot be achieved by a few on behalf of many". Creating consistently high quality service is harder than creating high quality product. High quality product is almost always produced in the privacy of your premises where errors or mistakes can be dealt with, without the customer ever learning about them.

However, the provision of service is almost always done with the customer watching, waiting and often disgruntled. Add to this the fact that requests or demands for service can come at any time, in any quantity, for an almost limitless number of reasons and we start to see why the achievement of consistently high quality customer service is not something that can be done easily in any business.

Parting Note:–

Building a customer's confidence in the organisation can take years, destroying it takes only minutes.

◎ – My next goal in this area is . . .

☎ – Who should I communicate my thoughts to?

NOTES

Key:

£ = Is there a way, I can help to increase company profits. Either by
     encouraging customers to buy more or by saving money?

◎ = My next goal in this area is . . .

⊂⊃⊃⊃ = Where do I fit in to this chain of events?

☎ = Who should I communicate my thoughts to?

? = Do I fully understand how this works and how it applies to me?

↘ = Ideas and suggestions I have for improvements

♄ = Is anything stopping/hindering my progress

<u>NOTES</u>

The Benefits

THE BENEFITS

There are enormous benefits to be gained from the provision of high quality service to a satisfied customer base.

However, the single largest problem faced by most companies is the fact that many of the benefits seem intangible. Often, in order to implement changes in the way a company operates, a cost justification has to be produced. One of the purposes of this guide is to help you cost justify statements such as the following:–

The benefits to be gained from providing a quality service to our customers are:–

* Our Company image is improved:

  By our Customers, potential Customers and our own staff.

* Customers are retained for longer:

  Once they have received and consistently receive good service they are more likely to stay loyal. A repeat sale is easier than a new one.

  Fewer complaints will result, and they are likely to be rectified more quickly and more cheaply.

* Staff are retained for longer:

  They feel happier in their jobs and are more committed and motivated to do a good job, increasing productivity and performance.

  They become easier to manage and are more likely to stay longer, reducing the costs and overheads of replacement.

*   Suppliers become more committed:

They want not only to share in the success, but will profit from yours. This can be used as a strong negotiating position in the working partnership.

*   The longer term future of our company becomes safer:

Any business with a satisfied customer base, committed staff and management, coupled with supportive suppliers is more likely to succeed and be amongst the winners of tomorrow.

Now make a quick guess at the following:–

The improved company image gains one extra new
customer this year, they will spend   £____

One customer who is not lost this year will spend   £____

One member of staff will not leave and need
replacing this year (advertising/interviewing/
training costs saved)   £____

1% extra discount is negotiated with your major
supplier because you are such a prestigious
reference customer (savings)   £____

                                      Total   £____

Parting note:–

A company with 100 customers, who contact them once a quarter, for a reason other than sales, where two staff are involved with each contact, is already spending

100 (customers) × 4 (contacts per year) × 2 (staff) × £10 (minimum cost for an employee to do anything)
= £8000 per annum on customer service regardless of the quality

? – Do I fully understand how this works and how it applies to me?
£ – Is there a way I can increase profits?

Page 15

NOTES

Key:
£ = Is there a way, I can help to increase company profits. Either by encouraging customers to buy more or by saving money?
◎ = My next goal in this area is . . .
☎ = Where do I fit in to this chain of events?
☎ = Who should I communicate my thoughts to?
? = Do I fully understand how this works and how it applies to me?
↘ = Ideas and suggestions I have for improvements
✋ = Is anything stopping/hindering my progress

NOTES

<u>NOTES</u>

The Customer

THE CUSTOMER

Today's more demanding customer expects product and service delivery faster, better, and in tune with his exact requirements.

Customers evaluate service quality with different standards than those applied to the product. A service is an intangible. It is the recollection of the transaction, not just the product purchased, but the experience of being served and served well. Both are important – equally so – to the customer's decision to do business with you and your organisation again.

Most companies invest vast amounts of money in gaining new business, equally vast amounts of money in the perfection and enhancement of their products – and next to nothing protecting their investment.

To put a real value on providing customer service you must first be able to value your customers. Having done this, it then becomes relatively straightforward to calculate the cost of losing customers and therefore, justify the costs involved with keeping them.

No matter what the size of your company, there are some simple calculations you can do to understand the direct costs involved with gaining new business, compared with the costs of retaining existing customers.

Try this calculation:

Divided by: $\dfrac{\text{(Salesperson Salary} + \text{Commission} + \text{Advertising} + \text{Marketing etc)}}{\text{Total number of new customers in a twelve month period}}$

Equals = £x, the cost of each new customer

Depending on the nature of your business there will also be a lead time associated with gaining new business. From this you can see that in order to keep one customer, it is worth spending almost any amount that is less than £x per annum.

£ – Is there a way to increase company profits?
coco – Where do I fit in to this chain of events?
☝ – Is anything stopping/hindering my progress?

Page 17

This is not to say that Sales and Marketing are no longer necessary. On the contrary, they will build a bigger, more profitable business in gaining new customers rather than constantly trying to replace lost customers.

Having a significant amount of major customers protects you against the impact of losing a customer. The larger your customer base the more you are protected against events outside your control.

Every customer has a turnover value. Whether you expect repeat business every week, month, or every ten years. If your customers are happy with the service you provide, this repeat business will come to you automatically, and can therefore be valued according to the life expectancy of a customer.

A simple record, similar to the example shown here, will help you to respond correctly to a customer.

CUSTOMER RECORD

CUSTOMER NAME:_____ CUSTOMER REF:_____
CONTACT NAME:_____ PHONE No: _____
OTHER USEFUL INFORMATION:_____
_____

VALUE: £_____PER:_____COST TO REPLACE:_____

*SENSITIVE: YES/NO

PREVIOUS CUSTOMER CONTACTS:

DATE	SUBJECT	REASON	ACTION	SATISFIED

*A sensitive customer is one who has recently experienced a poor quality product or service from your company and you feel needs to be nurtured back to satisfaction!

We must accept, that as perfection does not exist anywhere, mistakes will still happen.

↘ – Ideas and suggestions I have for improvements
☎ – Who should I communicate my thoughts to?

If you unfortunately jeopardise this life expectancy, by not treating the customer in the manner they expect, you cannot depend on their continued valuable business.

The cost to your company is the amount of money you would lose, if the service to the customer is poor and they do not stay loyal.

People who are in direct contact with customers should treat every one as if they are the most valuable.

The short and long term worth of a customer is a valuable piece of information, and can be used to help justify service improvements. The financial value of a customer can be usefully taken into consideration, if a situation arises where you need to spend money in order to achieve customer satisfaction. The question is, will it cost less to satisfy this customer than it will cost us to replace him? How much money will we lose if we lose this customer?

Parting note:–

You may sometimes find it difficult to believe, but customers are human beings too!

If their car didn't start, or their children are ill, or their boss has just shouted at them, you may be the first person they can take it out on. Whatever your feelings remember, YOU ARE PLEASED TO BE ABLE TO HELP THEM.

NOTES

Key:

£ = Is there a way, I can help to increase company profits. Either by encouraging customers to buy more or by saving money?

◎ = My next goal in this area is . . .

⊂⊐⊐⊐ = Where do I fit in to this chain of events?

☎ = Who should I communicate my thoughts to?

? = Do I fully understand how this works and how it applies to me?

⟍ = Ideas and suggestions I have for improvements

☝ = Is anything stopping/hindering my progress

NOTES

<u>NOTES</u>

The Service

THE SERVICE

Successful organisations achieve service quality through a commitment to excellence, not only from raw materials, production, marketing, sales and systems, but also people.

The company must examine its interactions with the customer from the customer's perspective, and then and only then, can it develop procedures that capitalise on and enhance the service experience.

Customer service is not simply a slogan. It must be an organisation-wide, visible commitment that concentrates the organisation's resources, and its ethos, to one end – Customer Satisfaction.

From the very top of the organisation everyone must understand the nature of the customers' experience. They must generate positive strategies and tactics to maximise the quality of that experience. This will improve the chances of increasing profitability.

Are your customers able to speak to you? Do you make it easy for them to do so? Do you encourage feedback, especially complaints?

Systems and procedures must be designed to serve the customer, not the internal convenience of the organisation and its structure.

This often means turning the whole organisation into a customer driven business entity.

↳ – Ideas and suggestions I have for improvements
? – Do I fully understand how this works and how it applies to me?
♥ – Is anything stopping/hindering my progress?

Page 23

LOOK LIVELY SID HERE COMES ANOTHER DISSATISFIED PUNTER ...

The following things can be addressed by any company at any time and at NO COST.

Make sure your customers are aware of

1. How to obtain service

2. What levels of service to expect

3. How you handle a request for service

4. Usual feedback/response times

5. How proud you are of your products and the service you offer

6. Your company's commitment to high quality service

Parting note:-

Service is a recollection, a memory, an experience – as such it has life only in the minds of your customers. Keep it simple, keep it honest, keep it willing and your customers will think highly of you, for years to come.

◎ – My next goal in this area is . . .
☎ – Who should I communicate my thoughts to?

<u>NOTES</u>

Key:
£ = Is there a way, I can help to increase company profits. Either by encouraging customers to buy more or by saving money?

◎ = My next goal in this area is . . .

☍☍ = Where do I fit in to this chain of events?

☎ = Who should I communicate my thoughts to?

? = Do I fully understand how this works and how it applies to me?

↘ = Ideas and suggestions I have for improvements

✋ = Is anything stopping/hindering my progress

<u>NOTES</u>

The Staff

The Staff

THE STAFF

This chapter is applicable to everyone. If you deal with customers on a daily basis some of the items mentioned may be familiar to you. However, if you deal with other members of staff they are your "Customers" and everything here applies to the way you deal with them.

Remember: "Quality Customer Service is the responsibility of everyone."

Making it obvious to the customer that staff are really trying to help them resolve their problems, requires many skills. Staff in this position must have the full support and backing of the whole organisation in assisting them. They are key members of staff and should realise what the customer expects of them as a service provider:

All staff should:

– Know who their customers are.

– Understand the impact of the problem on the customer's business or on them as human beings.

– Listen to the customers and work for them in resolving the query.

– Make customers feel comfortable and confident. They must trust what they are told.

– Not make promises that cannot be kept.

– Be positive, responsive and responsible.

– Be helpful and reasonable.

– Follow through to ensure that the customers have been satisfied.

? – Do I fully understand how this works and how it applies to me?
◎ – My next goal in this area is . . .

Page 27

– Never use excuses. Give valid reasons.

– Be honest and do everything within their power to satisfy the customer.

– Be polite and courteous.

Staff should have appropriate resources in terms of systems and procedures, for them to access relevant information quickly. This helps reduce the time wasted whilst customers may be waiting for a response. The customers feel more confident if they are getting the personal touch from someone who knows what they are talking about.

There should be mechanisms which enable staff to pass information about service call history and profiles throughout the organisation chain. This is more than simply passing statistics to see how busy they are, but should be used by management to identify areas of weakness. These areas will almost certainly directly impact profits.

Staff must have the power to escalate problems up the chain quickly if a given situation arises. They have been given the responsibility of responding to customers, which must be matched by an appropriate level of authority to get the job done, to the satisfaction of the customer. The decision making and escalation procedures should be designed to be simple, responsive and clearly understood by everyone. Remember the costs of gaining new customers will outweigh the costs of providing quality service to existing customers.

All these things are important to ensure that staff dealing directly with the customer, within the organisation, are given every help to succeed at every opportunity.

£ – Is there a way to increase company profits?
ꝏ – Where do I fit in to this chain of events?
☞ – Is anything stopping/hindering my progress?

AND IF I REMEMBER CORRECTLY THIS IS
WHERE MY CUSTOMER SERVICES DEPT IS...

Parting note:–

If the picture on the previous page reminds you of your company's Customer Service area, you are greatly reducing your chances of increasing profits.

⌐ – Ideas and suggestions I have for improvements
☏ – Who should I communicate my thoughts to?

NOTES

Key:

£ = Is there a way, I can help to increase company profits. Either by encouraging customers to buy more or by saving money?

◎ = My next goal in this area is . . .

⊂⊐⊐⊃ = Where do I fit in to this chain of events?

☎ = Who should I communicate my thoughts to?

? = Do I fully understand how this works and how it applies to me?

⟍ = Ideas and suggestions I have for improvements

⍦ = Is anything stopping/hindering my progress

NOTES

"Perceptions", "Expectations" and "Attitudes"

"PERCEPTIONS", "EXPECTATIONS" AND "ATTITUDES"

Why is it that sometimes, despite everyone in your organisation doing absolutely everything possible, to satisfy a customer, you fail?

"Perceptions", "Expectations", and "Attitudes"

Taking these words one at a time and starting with the dictionary definition:–

"Perception" – Insight or Intuition

– The way an organism detects and interprets information.

When two people are involved in one situation they will often have a very different view of that situation.

It is, therefore, possible for you to believe, beyond a shadow of a doubt, that the service you have provided to a customer has been exceptional.

However, your customer may have a totally different perception of that service.

Study the picture on the next page for a moment:

ᴄᴏᴏᴅ – Where do I fit in to this chain of events?
◎ – My next goal in this area is . . .

Page 31

The customer's perception:–

"I have received the wrong product, it is not at all suitable. I am now running out of time and patience – DO SOMETHING NOW!"

The supplier's perception:–

"We delivered on time <u>AND</u> we have sent you more expensive goods for which there will be no extra charge."

The lesson to be learned is: don't assume you know what the customer wants. 70% of the time you will be wrong.

"Expectation" – something looked forward to

– an attitude of hope.

Here is another area where minor misunderstanding can turn into major disasters, quickly and often very simply.

When a customer contacts you, they will often have already decided, in their own mind, what they expect you to do. This customer expectation is rarely passed on to you. However, if you do not meet it, the customer may well conclude that you have failed.

Study the picture on the next page for a moment:

? – Do I fully understand how this works and how it applies to me?
🖐 – Is anything stopping/hindering my progress?

Page 33

The customer's expectation:–

"Immediately – means now. I am freezing to death in shark infested waters, but it's O.K., the survival kit should be here any second now."

The supplier's expectation:–

"Immediately – we have done well today. Every order we have received has been made up and posted – no backlog. Even the order to the North Pole will be there by next Tuesday – the customer will be pleased."

The lesson learned is: you must find out as soon as a customer contacts you what they expect to happen.

Customer expectations, once revealed can, by careful handling, be changed and adjusted even totally reset. However, if you don't know what a customer expects, you have little or no chance of doing the right thing.

Ask and the customer will always tell you. Don't ask and you will fail.

"Attitude" – a mental view or disposition

– a position of the body indicating mood or emotion

Regardless of the information you need to give a customer, good news, bad news, no news, your attitude will have a greater impact than the news itself.

Study the picture on the next page for a moment:

Here are some basic guidelines that you should keep in mind at all times, when dealing with customers and usually when you are dealing with other members of staff.

Smile but don't laugh

Sound concerned but not worried

Be interested but not chatty

Reflect urgency but not panic

Be confident but not arrogant

Sound polite but not patronising

Be firm but not bossy

Above all be proud of yourself, your products and your company.

Parting note:–

The total cost of implementing everything in this chapter throughout your entire company is:–

£0.00 inc VAT

The potential increase in profits is unlimited.

☏ – Who should I communicate my thoughts to?
◎ – My next goal in this area is . . .

Page 37

NOTES

Key:

£ = Is there a way, I can help to increase company profits. Either by encouraging customers to buy more or by saving money?

◎ = My next goal in this area is . . .

ⅭⅭⅭⅭ = Where do I fit in to this chain of events?

☏ = Who should I communicate my thoughts to?

? = Do I fully understand how this works and how it applies to me?

↳ = Ideas and suggestions I have for improvements

↯ = Is anything stopping/hindering my progress

<u>NOTES</u>

<u>NOTES</u>

Measurement and Monitoring

MEASUREMENT AND MONITORING

The service you provide <u>must</u> be measurable. You cannot improve that which you cannot measure.

-   Record all and every contact with customers, use codes to speed up the process and help with analysis.

-   Maintain History Records. Regularly analyse and review cause and effect.

-   Verify and regularly check information recorded on the customer, and their needs against current requirements.

-   Check whether the customer is satisfied with a solution, answer, or piece of information and record this information for analysis.

-   Constantly review the amount of contact with customers about specific issues to determine changing trends in the market place. Act on these changes and prepare to deal with them more effectively next time they happen.

A simple record similar to the one shown on the next page will help you record customer contacts.

CONTACT RECORD

CALLER NAME:_____ PHONE No._____

COMPANY NAME:_____

CUSTOMER REFERENCE:_____NEXT ACTION DATE TIME:

_____/_____/_____ _____:_____

_____/_____/_____ _____:_____

DETAILS:_____

UPDATES

WHEN   SUBJECT   REASON   ACTION   NOTES

CLOSING INFORMATION FOR ANALYSIS:

CUSTOMER REFERENCE_____

SUBJECT_____

REASON_____

ACTION_____

SATISFIED Y/N/DON'T KNOW_____

DATE CLOSED ___/___/___

NB (Never write anything derogatory about a customer – they may see it)

Having said that, it is vital to record information. Care must be taken to avoid over-complicating the process.

Staff dealing with customers must focus on the customer and not on the information gathering mechanism.

Any measurement or monitoring system must provide the information you need quickly, and allow information to be recorded quickly. The system used should be:

– Simple

Staff and customers will participate more readily, quickly and effectively, if the system is simple.

– Balanced

A balance needs to be maintained, which avoids the information being so simple as to be worthless, or being so complicated as to hamper participation.

– Honest

The system should be designed to encourage the customer to be open and honest about criticism.

There is a trade-off between speed, simplicity and the amount and value of information gathered.

If the picture on the next page reminds you of your company, then you are spending more time and money on information gathering, than you are on creating customer satisfaction!

£ – Is there a way to increase company profits?
♥ – Is anything stopping/hindering my progress?

Page 41

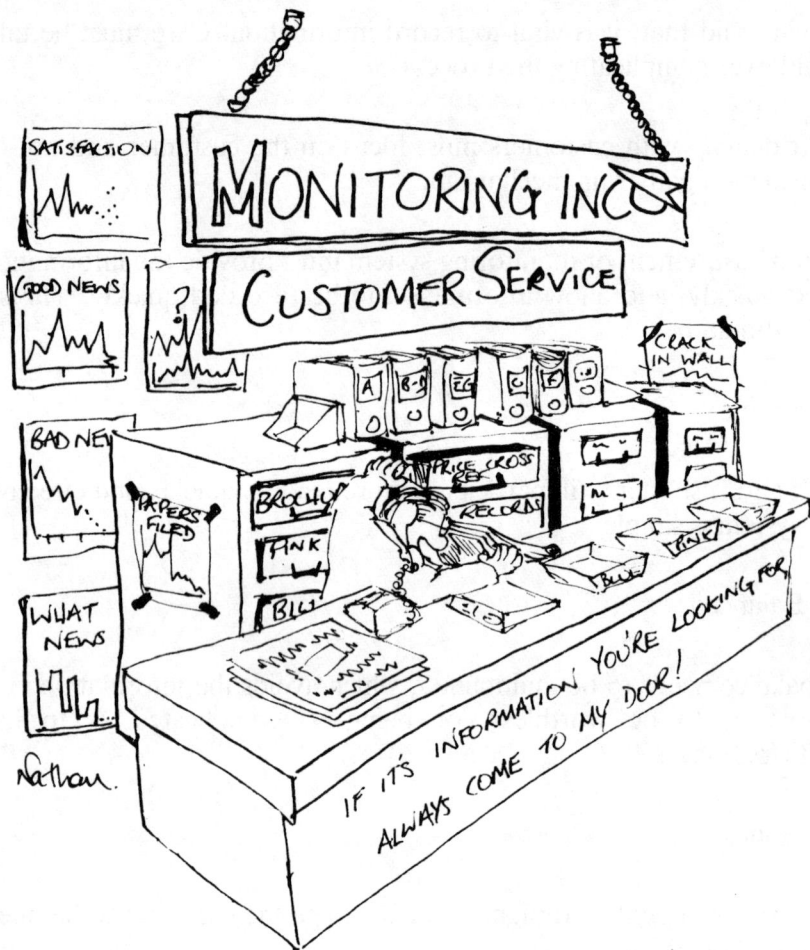

Parting note:–

Research has proved that service providers who guess, will, in 70+% of all instances:–

a. *Name the loudest and most unpleasant customer as the one who makes the most contacts.*

b. *Name as the cause of the majority of contacts, the subject they either know least about or have the greatest problem handling.*

◎ – My next goal in this area is . . .
☏ – Who should I communicate my thoughts to?

Page 43

<u>NOTES</u>

Key:
£ = Is there a way, I can help to increase company profits. Either by encouraging customers to buy more or by saving money?
◎ = My next goal in this area is . . .
☎ = Where do I fit in to this chain of events?
☎ = Who should I communicate my thoughts to?
? = Do I fully understand how this works and how it applies to me?
↲ = Ideas and suggestions I have for improvements
♛ = Is anything stopping/hindering my progress

<u>NOTES</u>

<u>NOTES</u>

Reactive Customer Service

REACTIVE CUSTOMER SERVICE

Let's start with the dictionary definition

REACTIVE – To respond to an action or stimulus

– The reciprocal action of two things acting together

Customer service organisations and departments are reacting to contacts from customers as a matter of course; either by telephone, letter or face to face. Simply putting customer service staff in this position, is on its own, not enough. It is also about how efficiently these contacts are handled, and how easy it is for the customer to get to the right person, to solve their problem or answer the query.

With the best will in the world, no company will ever be able to foresee all that is required of them by their customers.

However, there are many many simple things which start to cause customer dissatisfaction. A large number of these can be addressed quickly and easily.

CXED – Where do I fit in to this chain of events?
? – Do I fully understand how this works and how it applies to me?

Page 45

How many times does the phone ring before it is answered?
(Set a maximum and try to avoid going beyond it)

Are the telephones often engaged?
(Check by getting someone to regularly telephone you in known busy periods)

How many times does a customer have to explain why they are calling?
(If you pass a call on, ensure all the information you have already been told is known to the next person)

Do you call customers back before they have to call you again?
(Keep a record for a week or two, then aim to improve on that result)

How are the customers greeted and addressed?
(The first caller of the day and the last caller of the day must get the same high standard)

Do customers get the undivided attention they deserve, every time?
(Never chat to other members of staff, try to read something, listen to another conversation or fill in the pools form when on the telephone to a customer, you WILL miss something important)

The Reactive process diagram

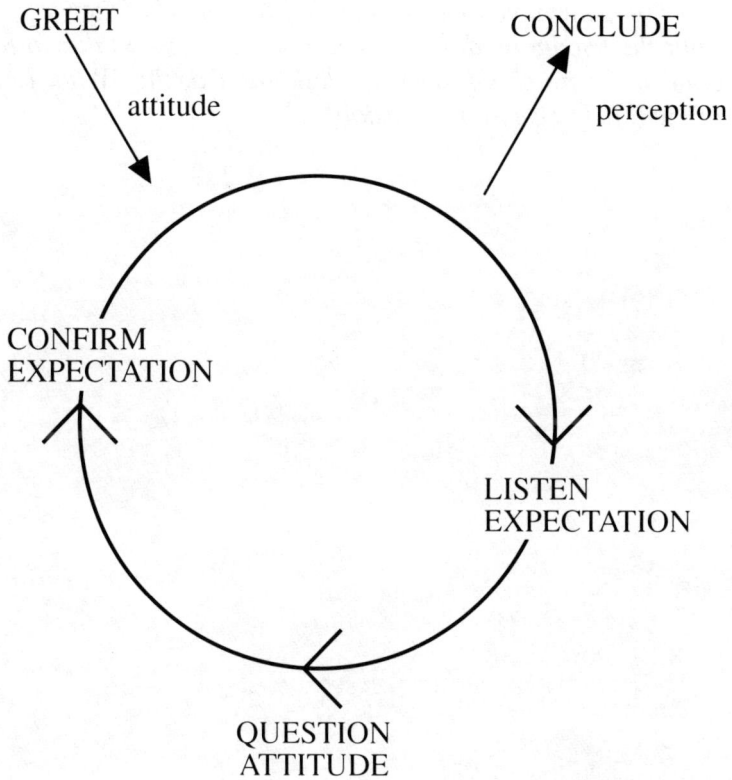

GREET

attitude

CONCLUDE

perception

CONFIRM
EXPECTATION

LISTEN
EXPECTATION

QUESTION
ATTITUDE

During the reactive phase of your contact with a customer you are responsible for:

Your attitude

Revealing their expectations

Influencing their perceptions

Parting note:–

Whilst customer service is often reactive, you should never react to a customer in a negative or rude way, no matter what they say. When you have put the telephone down, if you are feeling stress due to high levels of self control – a notebook on your desk entitled, the "What I really wanted to say" will help release the tension!

NOTES

Key:

£ = Is there a way, I can help to increase company profits. Either by encouraging customers to buy more or by saving money?

◎ = My next goal in this area is . . .

ᴄᴏᴏᴏ = Where do I fit in to this chain of events?

☏ = Who should I communicate my thoughts to?

? = Do I fully understand how this works and how it applies to me?

↘ = Ideas and suggestions I have for improvements

✦ = Is anything stopping/hindering my progress

<u>NOTES</u>

Pro-active Customer
Service

PRO-ACTIVE CUSTOMER SERVICE

Pro   – Before in time or position
       – Forward

Active – Moving, working, doing
       – Busy or involved in

Regardless of how polished your reactive service is, without pro-activity the quality of that service will occasionally remain the same, but usually slip slowly downhill.

This is possibly one of the least understood areas and therefore the most threatening to you and your company.

It is reasonable to say that we all live in an ever changing and advancing world. As individuals, our needs and tastes change constantly.

This is equally true of a company; products, services, prices and availability, will change. Combine this with similar levels of change in your customers' requirements and you have an ever evolving service cycle.

Common problem areas are:–

1. New product launches are not communicated to everyone in advance.

2. Changes in company procedures being revealed to service providers after implementation.

3. The assumption that a previously satisfied customer will be equally pleased if the last solution is duplicated.

4. Assuming there will not be any impact on your customers, from changes you make to a product or operation which seem to you to be minor.

In fact this list is endless, for every business it will vary slightly. However the root of the majority of problems are two-fold.

    i. Lack of communication, through your company and throughout your customer base.

Much worse and more frequent

    ii. A lack of response or action to readily available information.

The biggest crime you or your company can commit in the eyes of a customer is having a known problem and failing to act on it.

Having understood this, it is relatively simple and inexpensive to rectify this type of problem.

Information that could affect the quality of service you and your company provides must be freely available to everyone, as far in advance as possible.

£ – Is there a way to increase company profits?

 – Is anything stopping/hindering my progress?

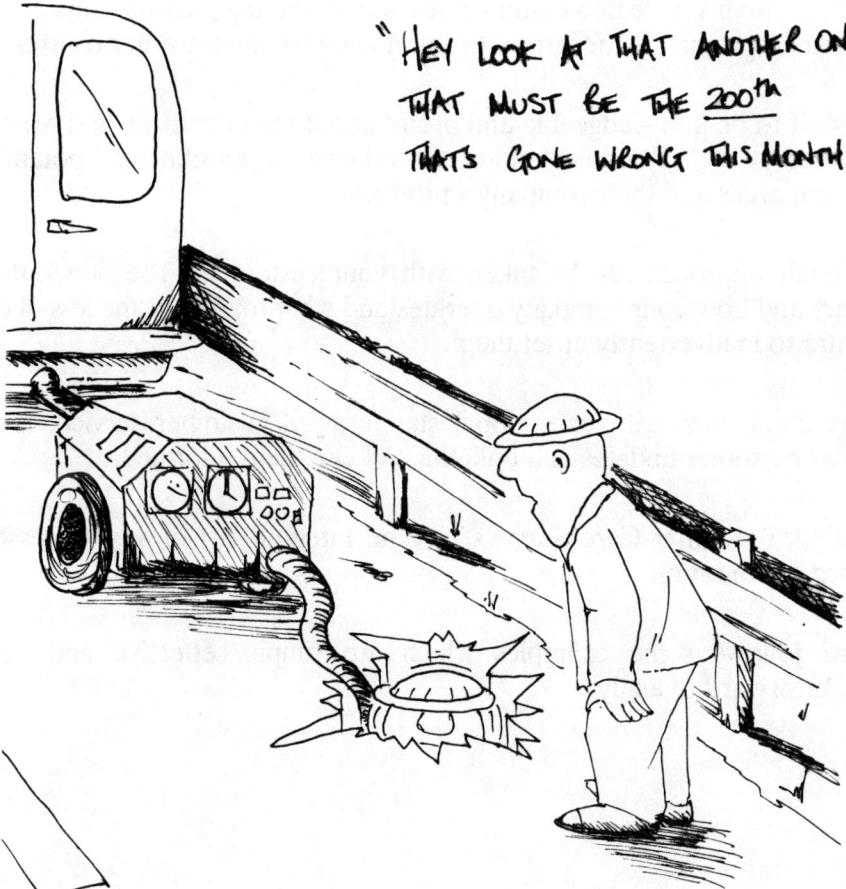

The vehicles for information dispersal may vary dramatically. Often these can be company wide newsletters, sales and marketing presentations to key personnel, product demonstrations, brief training and refresher courses.

For staff to be knowledgeable and proud about their company and what it sells, they MUST understand each other's responsibilities, potential problem areas and their company's products.

A similar approach can be taken with your customers. The better they understand how your company operates and what to expect, the less likely you are to inadvertently upset them.

Many companies with exceptional standards of customer service, issue regular customer updates and bulletins to keep them informed.

Finally, "Customer Care Surveys" are an integral part of any successful service organisation.

There follows some examples which are simple, effective and very straightforward to analyse.

◎ – My next goal in this area is . . .
☏ – Who should I communicate my thoughts to?

CUSTOMER SURVEY

DO YOU FIND THE SERVICE WE PROVIDE . . .

Excellent	Good	Poor	Very Poor
[ ]	[ ]	[ ]	[ ]
4	3	2	1

ARE THE STAFF USUALLY POLITE?

Yes [ ] No [ ]
1 0

DO WE DO WHAT WE SAY WE WILL DO?

Always	Usually	Not Often	Never
[ ]	[ ]	[ ]	[ ]
4	3	2	1

ANY OTHER COMMENTS?

We welcome honest criticism in our pursuit of service excellence.
Please feel free to comment:

_____

_____

_____

Company Name: _____ Telephone No.: _____

Contact Name: _____ Job Title: _____

Address: _____

Address: _____

County: _____ Post Code: _____

This is a very basic set of questions that could be sent to any customer.

Based on this style you can develop your own survey forms but remember to keep them simple, your customers are very busy people. Using numbered boxes helps in the analysis of returns. Remember, management should elevate analysis over internal concensus.

If you would like the customers to help you improve your service, the same style can be used to gather information.

Another style of questioning: Does it meet the need? What is different this month from last month? Are you, the customer satisfied? If not, why not? What can we do to improve? What do we do well? What do we do badly?

Customer Survey

How can we improve our service to you?

Faster Response Times   [ ]

More Knowledgeable Staff   [ ]

Extended Customer Service Hours [ ]

Please put the above in priority sequence – 1 – 2 – 3

We welcome honest criticism in our pursuit of service excellence.
Please feel free to comment:

....

....

Many thanks for your help.

Again, this style of questioning is easy for the customer to follow and very simple for you to analyse.

It is always worth putting two or three lines on the bottom of any survey form for additional comments.

If you send the questionnaires to customers and they do not return them – TELEPHONE – you may think they have nothing to say and believe your service is beyond improvement.

However, they may just be going somewhere else!

Sample surveys are a good method of extracting useful information about your customers, and they enable you to make changes in line with their comments and expectations, but you need not survey each and every customer. It may be more appropriate to canvas them on a geographic basis, by product type, by problem type, by spend etc, etc . . .

With a need to keep 'your eye on the ball', service level measurement is essential. They should be constantly reviewed and ask yourself 'How well are we doing?' The service objectives can only be maintained if service levels are measured. Speedy reaction in implementing changes to the strategy are essential and should be constantly reviewed and enhanced, based on customer feedback.

Parting note:–

Be Warned

This aspect of service is simple, straightforward and relatively inexpensive. If done properly, it will improve customer loyalty and repeat business.

However, done badly it can produce negative results.

Ask and you will be told
Ignore the responses and your customers will assume you have failed.

◎ – My next goal in this area is . . .
☏ – Who should I communicate my thoughts to?

Page 55

NOTES

Key:

£ = Is there a way, I can help to increase company profits. Either by encouraging customers to buy more or by saving money?

◎ = My next goal in this area is . . .

co℠o = Where do I fit in to this chain of events?

☎ = Who should I communicate my thoughts to?

? = Do I fully understand how this works and how it applies to me?

↘ = Ideas and suggestions I have for improvements

✌ = Is anything stopping/hindering my progress

NOTES

NOTES

The Answer

THE ANSWER

If you have turned to this section hoping that it will give you one simple, straightforward, once only, solution to high quality Customer Service and through this, increased profits then you will be disappointed.

The good news is, over 75% of high quality service provision will cost nothing to implement in real cash. There is a cost to the people involved. It is commitment, dedication and hard work in conjunction with a real desire to achieve.

Organisations which achieve service delivery excellence, adopt similar customer care techniques and practices:

They have VISION – a developed and evolving strategy for service which is clearly and consistently communicated from the top of the organisation.

They have VISIBLE MANAGEMENT who cultivate open and honest communication between internal service groups, staff, management and their customers.

Service and service quality is openly discussed and ENCOURAGED at all levels of the organisation.

They have customer oriented, service delivery systems that have the PERSONAL TOUCH.

They hire, train, promote and motivate the service culture THROUGH-OUT the organisation.

They MARKET service quality to their customers and employees.

They set employee objectives and openly REWARD quality service delivery and achievement.

---

ccoo – Where do I fit in to this chain of events?
ᒌ – Ideas and suggestions I have for improvements
Page 57

The managers are there to serve the staff – to make it easier for them to do their jobs well.

There are no mysteries involved and research shows ANY business can achieve quality Customer Service. When YOU DO, then you will find your rewards in increased profitability.

Parting note:–

"Quality of Service is not achieved by few on behalf of many."

£ – Is there a way to increase company profits?
☎ – Who should I communicate my thoughts to?
✋ – Is anything stopping/hindering my progress?

NOTES

Key:

£ = Is there a way, I can help to increase company profits. Either by encouraging customers to buy more or by saving money?

◎ = My next goal in this area is . . .

ᴄᴏᴏᴏ = Where do I fit in to this chain of events?

☎ = Who should I communicate my thoughts to?

? = Do I fully understand how this works and how it applies to me?

ᐅ = Ideas and suggestions I have for improvements

♨ = Is anything stopping/hindering my progress

NOTES

Final Thoughts

FINAL THOUGHTS

Providing good customer care can literally cost nothing and is the fastest route to increased profitability with relatively little or no outlay.

Improving Customer Service can be achieved by looking at the simple low or zero cost issues first. As customers we have all experienced the frustration, of feeling that we have not been carefully or well served. As a result we feel no obligation to return. Even worse, we tell everyone about our bad experiences. This negative marketing is very damaging and affects profitability. We should all try to convert the negative situation into a positive experience, by giving that little bit extra.

Lose a customer once and you will probably lose him for life!

A simple shift in attitude, which will cost nothing, will reap big rewards.

Consider how customers are addressed when interfacing with the frontline staff.

Think about how customers are greeted.

Give customers the undivided attention they deserve.

Make it easy for the customer to be directed to the right person.

Make it easy to contact your company.

Ensure telephones are not always engaged.

Do not keep customers waiting.

Companies spend sizeable proportions of their revenue on Marketing, Public Relations and Sales in the pursuit of new business.

It therefore seems appropriate to spend, not necessarily money, but at least time and effort in the objective of keeping current customers happy and ensuring their return. Satisfying customers is not just about product quality.

When considering your organisation and its customer base, do not just think of that customer as an individual. If they are getting good products and services then it is likely that their immediate family, friends, and working associates will get to know about it and also become customers. One 'quality' transaction could result in ten additional new customers.

Improving or instigating a customer care programme does not mean that a whole new structure has to be introduced with additional staff and costs.

By all means make someone responsible, but it is imperative that the whole organisation is aware of the concept. They must not only be aware, but understand the concept and why it exists.

"GIVING BAD CUSTOMER SERVICE COULD COST YOU THE COMPANY!"

DO'S AND DON'TS

Read the following Do's and Don'ts frequently. Ask yourself not only where do I do well, but also more importantly where and how can I improve?

SERVICE

DO

– it, if you say you will.

– ensure you understand what the customer requires.

– correct problem areas permanently.

– publish and ensure your customer understands how to get service.

– feed back service information to the business.

– be aware of previous information.

– be reliable and honest.

– strive to turn any contact with a customer into something positive.

DON'T

– do it fast if you are likely to get it wrong.

– assume an existing answer is right every time.

– quote rules and regulations that benefit your company.

– be distracted or indifferent to the customer's problem.

– ask the customer to call back (you will call them).

– promise what you cannot deliver.

STAFF

DO

– give reasons.

– admit you are wrong (if you are).

– make sure you understand your business and your products.

– what is possible now (be honest).

– treat the customer with respect (they will then respect you).

– manage all situations closely.

– listen, repeat and confirm to ensure you have understood the customer's requirements/expectations.

– ensure you adjust unrealistic expectations.

– remember the person on the phone indirectly pays your wages.

– be human (your customer is).

– make the customer feel they are the only person you are working for.

– be open and honest – never lie to a customer.

– be positive and enthusiastic.

◎ – My next goal in this area is . . .

DON'T

– give excuses.

– talk down to customers.

– contradict the customer (even if you think they are wrong).

– meddle.

– bring your moods or personal problems to work.

– be persuaded to offer unrealistic solutions or expectations.

– lose your temper or be indifferent.

– try to cover-up a mistake if you have made one.

CUSTOMERS

DO

– be obvious about your desire to improve the service.

– keep them informed.

– confirm the information gathered and tell them you are acting on it – and do it.

– encourage them to talk to you.

– maintain contact even if no new information is available.

– encourage them to contact you for good as well as bad reasons.

– start to build a relationship with them from the first contact.

– confirm and agree their expectations.

DON'T

– assume they know the answers.

– promise them what you cannot deliver.

– guess what they want, you will only be 30% right.

– ask for details on the telephone if you know you cannot help.

– ever keep them on hold on the telephone – call back.

– criticise your company, colleagues or products.

– say it's not my fault or my problem (you are representing your whole company).

Parting note:–

The Successful companies of tomorrow will achieve their success through a commitment to serving their customers.

If your company ignores this fact then it will not be amongst the companies of tomorrow.

Take notice and you may well be one of tomorrow's LEADERS.

A final thought from Nathan the cartoonist:–

If all else fails . . .

NOTES

Key:

£ = Is there a way, I can help to increase company profits. Either by encouraging customers to buy more or by saving money?

◎ = My next goal in this area is . . .

∞∞ = Where do I fit in to this chain of events?

☎ = Who should I communicate my thoughts to?

? = Do I fully understand how this works and how it applies to me?

✗ = Ideas and suggestions I have for improvements

✋ = Is anything stopping/hindering my progress

NOTES

The Company Commitment

THE COMPANY COMMITMENT

Customer service is not just aimed at changes to the way staff operate when dealing with customers. To succeed it must be driven and directed from the top, the very top of the organisation. Full commitment and support must be given, and be seen to be given to all staff members whether in direct contact with customers or not.

Each member of staff should be saying, when asked what their rôle in the organisation is:

"I am employed to improve customer service, but I work in accounts."

Quality Customer Service will increase profitability provided it is a total company responsibility. No one person in the company can ever say that Customer Service is the responsibility of someone else.

The whole ethos of the organisation must be geared towards customer satisfaction.

To improve or instigate customer service, a total company strategy must be adopted.

Very careful consideration should be given to solutions that apparently cost money over and above normal service costs. They are more likely in fact to make money and increase profits.

Apart from developing a strategy, staffing considerations must be taken into account, these should include:

∞∞ – Where do I fit in to this chain of events?
£ – Is there a way to increase company profits?

Page 67

The environment in which staff work

Product and Service Training

Team Building

Resourcing with appropriate equipment, procedures and systems

Simple, easy and clear communications

A clearly defined method of praise and reward

The right tools for the job

An honest approach

Remember an overriding key to your company success in Customer Service relies on this clear communication between all the involved parties:– and don't forget the customer is totally involved.

From original inception to a mature living organism, there is a need for communication throughout the organisation – up, down and sideways – from your suppliers and your customers.

It is easy to pay lip service to Customer Service

Parting note:–

Many companies have achieved greatness through service, your's can be one of them.

◎ – My next goal in this area is . . .
☏ – Who should I communicate my thoughts to?

NOTES

Key:

£ = Is there a way, I can help to increase company profits. Either by encouraging customers to buy more or by saving money?

◎ = My next goal in this area is . . .

⊂⊃⊃⊃ = Where do I fit in to this chain of events?

☎ = Who should I communicate my thoughts to?

? = Do I fully understand how this works and how it applies to me?

↖ = Ideas and suggestions I have for improvements

♉ = Is anything stopping/hindering my progress

NOTES

Appendix

The Ten Commandments

I *Involvement from all*

N *Never too busy*

C *Commitment to Customer Satisfaction*

R *Reliability*

E *Effective Customer Solutions*

A *Attitude to Service*

S *Sensitivity to the Customer Needs*

I *Initiative to resolve*

N *No lies*

G *Generation of Trust*

The 7 Deadly Sins

P *Procrastination*

R *Rudeness*

O *Obstructiveness*

F *Failure to give service*

I *Indifference*

T *Trivialisation*

S *Speculative Responses*

<u>NOTES</u>

Key:

£ = Is there a way, I can help to increase company profits. Either by encouraging customers to buy more or by saving money?

◎ = My next goal in this area is . . .

⊂⊃⊂⊃ = Where do I fit in to this chain of events?

☎ = Who should I communicate my thoughts to?

? = Do I fully understand how this works and how it applies to me?

↳ = Ideas and suggestions I have for improvements

♥ = Is anything stopping/hindering my progress

<u>NOTES</u>

<u>NOTES</u>

<u>NOTES</u>

<u>NOTES</u>

<u>NOTES</u>

<u>NOTES</u>

<u>NOTES</u>

<u>NOTES</u>

NOTES

NOTES

NOTES